Being Home

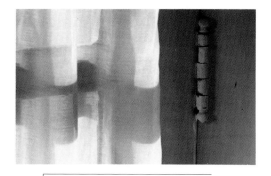

Being Home
A Book of Meditations

Gunilla Norris
Photographs by Greta D. Sibley

BELL TOWER   New York

Published by Bell Tower, an imprint of Harmony Books, a division of Crown Publishers, Inc., 201 East 50th Street, New York, New York 10022. Member of the Crown Publishing Group. HARMONY and colophon and BELL TOWER and colophon are trademarks of Crown Publishers, Inc.

Manufactured in the United States of America

Library of Congress Cataloging-in-Publication Data
Norris, Gunilla Brodde, 1939–
Being home: a book of meditations/ by Gunilla Norris; photographs by Greta D. Sibley. —1st ed.
p.   cm.
1. Devotional calendars. 2. Spiritual life. I. Title.
BL624.N67 1991
242—dc20
90-36976
CIP

ISBN 0-517-58159-0

10 9 8 7 6 5 4 3 2 1

First Edition

To the housekeeping spirit

Contents

Acknowledgments

We are grateful to friends and family who encouraged and sustained us through this project—especially those generous ones who took the time to respond to the manuscript, photographs, and design, and who helped bring this book to publication.

A special word of thanks to Norman Sibley, whose love, skill, and discrimination supported this book in an essential way.

Author's Preface

For twenty years now, I have been trying to write this book. It has been on bits and pieces of paper. It has moved with me from house to house in manila folders. It was on my mind and in my heart when I was in my twenties and newly married. It came back when my children went to school. It resurfaced when I went to work full time. Yet it is only now that I am nearly fifty years of age that I can conceive of writing it. I wonder why?

The children are grown. My twenty-eight-year marriage is over. I am living alone in a nineteenth-century farmhouse in Newtown, Connecticut, where I also work as a therapist. The book has turned up again and wants to be put down on paper. Maybe the book has been writing itself all along during these years. Maybe it is writing me...I don't know. In any case, there are not a lot of words to this book...but there is a central spirit, a kind of movement toward articulation, a brailling forward with or without words for a way to *be* in the extraordinary beauty of dailiness.

Prayer and housekeeping—they go together. They have always gone together. We simply know that our daily round *is* how we live. When we clean and order our homes, we are somehow also cleaning and ordering ourselves. We know this by virtue of being human creatures. How we hold the

simplest of our tasks speaks loudly about how we hold life itself.

How then do we "come home" spiritually and dwell there? In my own life I have found no better way than to value and savor the sacredness of daily living, to rely on repetition, that humdrum rhythm, which heals and steadies. Increasingly it is for me a matter of being willing "to be in place," to enter into deeper communion *with* the objects and actions of a day and to allow them to commune *with* me. It is a way to know and to be known...to surrender my isolation by participating in the experience as it happens. And it is a struggle! So often it is said that we teach what we want to learn. I want to learn this very much.

All of us have some kind of daily round. As human beings we have a strong intuition that deep within our dailiness lies meaning, a huge dimension. But how do we speak of that sense of the sacred? How do we address holiness? I have chosen to use words like *Life, Reality, Glory, Mystery*. For me they point to that which is fundamental and beyond knowing. I am truly helpless here and hope that you will forgive this very inadequate formulation. Personally I have been eased by using the simple word *You* when addressing the awesome mystery within and beyond my life. I do so in these prayers. In your reading, if

this is difficult for you, I invite you to find another word that works better.

In fact, this whole book is an invitation, an invitation to a process. It invites you to become aware of the prayers that you are already praying. Perhaps you will be surprised at how full of silent prayers your daily round is, how full of meaning and grace. It is my hope that together we will learn more about this.

In my own life, I discovered that certain moments in my day held meaning for me. I began to linger around them, to dwell with them. That is when I discovered that I was somehow praying. But I didn't know that before. I would return again and again to one task or moment until I could hear that prayer that was there. Then I would focus on some other moment. Over time, my tasks have slowly begun to recall me into living consciously more of the day. They are becoming my teachers.

You may want to choose one of these prayers and stay with your experience of the same activity in your life for a week or a month until something yields itself in you. Then you can add another activity until it too has become a prayer within you. Slowly, the most ordinary of days will start to become transparent, to shine with meaning.

Of course, the prayers change. It's not always the same thing dwelt with over the kitchen sink. Often the prayers are wordless. They are simply a kind of awareness, a return to gratitude, or to conscience, or to praise. Over time this way of linking what is at hand with what is in the heart can recall us into communing with the wonder and gift of the Presence in the present. Perhaps this will be so for you. And perhaps you will find something that is even more steadying, more your own expression. I wish it for you.

Gunilla Norris
Newtown, Connecticut

Photographer's Preface

I remember once being very small in a very large cathedral. The sun was powerful that day, so powerful that it created brilliant beams of color as it penetrated the thick stained-glass windows. I thought I was seeing the light of heaven. I suppose I was.

My mother and I were seated in a pew near the sanctuary. My father was far, far away, high up in the choir loft. He was playing the organ, deftly picking the right sounds out of the eight thousand pipes at his disposal. Two hands on different keyboards, both feet on the pedals, head nodding to cue the choir, eyes skipping from his music to the mirror set up to monitor movement in the sanctuary. My catechist had already succeeded in getting across the idea that merely being a body in a pew did not constitute attendance at Mass. One must be present. So I expressed concern to my mother: "If Dad is busy playing the organ, how can that count?"

She told me that every note he played was a prayer. I was impressed.

More recently I've rediscovered this simple truth in the care with which Buddhist monks prepare tea, in the joy of flower beds well tended, and in the simple act of ironing a shirt. If anything we do in this life matters, then *everything* we do matters. There isn't living and Living. The only difference is how

completely we *give* ourselves to living, how we let ourselves be part of the cosmos and be lived. There isn't light and Light, trash and Trash. There is no alternate utopia running parallel to this life. This is it.

The prayers in this book honor ordinary moments. I hope these photographs do so as well. I hope they sing the praises of light and shadow, shape, form, texture, and mood. I look to suspend time the way a dancer leaps into the air and hangs there for a moment. Then I want to move on, clean and sensitive as unexposed film.

Greta D. Sibley
North Eastham, Massachusetts

Introduction

Sometimes saying prayers keeps us from *being* prayers. Words come then not in response to life but in substitution for life. We think the map is the territory and we are untouched by the smells and wonders of actual living. For me the orientation that I want to embrace more and more is toward receiving my life, toward a continual intention to make room for Mystery's way within me. I don't think we can go deeply into ourselves—but Life seeking itself can go deeply in us. We can be infused, loved, and fathomed by it. And when we are, we cannot help but sing out our joy. We need that activity in us to *be* ourselves....

I once witnessed this ecstatic process in a small human creature. I was at the beach, walking along the water's edge when a young child ran on very unsteady legs into the water. It was the infant's intensity that caught my attention. I looked for the mother. She was some distance away and seemed comfortable enough about her child's safety not to interfere with what was happening.

The child, a boy with wet sagging diapers, ran into the water with that half-weaving, half-stumbling motion of infants who have just learned to walk. I first thought he would fall, and then that he would not stop until he was in over his head. But this child knew when he was in deep enough.

Seeing him with the Long Island Sound lapping against his chubby thighs, I realized that from his perspective these small waves were giants. He was with something VERY BIG.

His small body was intense with concentration. He was thrumming like an instrument, standing there in the water. Then he turned and, still deep in the experience, walked unsteadily out of the water and over the thin strip of pebbles at the water's edge. Then he made a kind of circle and went right back into the water up to his thighs for another experience of *sea*. He did this perhaps seven or eight times, as if verifying what this wet, cold living thing called water was to him.

I could feel the high excitement of his experience even yards away from him. Finally, fully satisfied, he stood in his wet diapers and began an unintelligible but eloquent speech to the water, to the gulls, to the sand, to the world. This baby was obviously not yet speaking with words, but he was certainly speaking with his heart. The sound was beautiful. He was tell-singing his experience with arms outflung. It was a deep burble—a joyful noise to the Lord!

Only after naming his experience in his own personal language did he notice me noticing him.

A shy look came over his face, and he did a fast exit out of the water, over the pebble strip—and then around back into the water, finishing with his speech gurgled at the top of his voice. The smile on his face and the sidelong look he gave me told me that he knew we both knew what all this felt like, including the joys of repetition. We were in this together!

We are in this world together. Greta and I offer this book to you, to each other, and to the Glory we all live in. We hope that in the repetition of intention to remain open in our daily round we will come to feel how VERY BIG is the depth of Life even in the smallest of activities. We trust that we are intended for ecstasy, that each day we are meant to be steeped in mystery, and so to *remember* our true lives. Then we will not be able to stop the natural response—the living of praise.

Being Home

Awakening

First thought—as in "first light"—
let me be aware that I waken *in* You.
Before I even think that I am in my bed,
let me think that I am *in* You.

Eyes crusted over, mouth dry,
my creature self feels so inert and dumb.
Let me be aware that these words
searching toward You into consciousness
are also coming from You.

You are waking me out of this sleepiness
into awareness that my life, my thoughts,
my body, my tasks, my loves, passions,
and sorrows are gifts from You,
to be discovered and received this day.

Each hour wake me further to find You.
Let me relish in You, exult in You,
play in You, be faithful in You.
Let me be wholly present
to living the gift of time.

Help me to feel that tremendous, unrelenting joy
which is Your constancy
and which will not let any of us go.
Wake me to You.

Standing

This morning as I put my feet on the floor
let me remember how many thousands of years
it took for this act to be possible—
the slow and painstaking development
so that a human creature could rise,
could stand on two feet, and then walk.

From the very beginning, from the first explosion
Your precise and patient love has been creating us.

The wonder is that now my hands are free
even as I walk or run or stand or dance.
The wonder is that now while I am upright,
my eyes can gaze at the ground,
along the ground, and beyond to the horizon....

I know You have made me
and all creatures for freedom...
an ever-increasing, evolving freedom.
I am filled with awe by this.
It requires that we face the unknown,
that we rise to it.
You are still exploding in us
and I am scared.
My trust is so puny.

But You are near. You are here
even as You have been from the very first.
You are the vast time and space
in which life is happening. You are Life itself
providing us with centuries to become
Your conscious image.

With wonder at what You have entrusted to us,
help me to know that You are both
the ground and the being
apart from which there is nothing.
Help me to stand up
in Your freedom.

Walking

I leave the bedroom...I begin walking
through my house. I will traverse it
many times today like a creature
covering her turf. It is a journey
that zigzags and returns upon itself...
a circumambulation...a re-remembering of "place."

I know this is the way many ancients prayed—
circling a holy site to deepen their devotion.
I wonder if animals offer their speechless prayers to You
by scudding over their well-known ground?

My foot rises. Before it falls
there is a tiny moment when
neither of my feet are really carrying weight—
a suspension, a moment of physical trust.
Something in me knows
that the ground will still be there.
Let me return to this innate knowledge—
this ancient confidence.

The floor in this house is wood...wide, old boards.
When I walk I am walking on the wood and in the woods.
I am walking on the life of these trees.
They have been cut and planed...offered up
for this sheltering. Let me remember to offer myself
to be shelter for something in Your world.

My foot falls. The ground rises to meet it.
A holy, ordinary moment is repeating itself.
All the time I am meeting and being met like this.
Your whole creation is ground.
Help me to remember that in this mutuality
we can become home for each other.
You are asking us slowly to become
Your holy site.

Washing

Water runs over my hands.
Water covers my face.

Inside, my body consists mostly of water,
the way the globe, too, consists mostly of water.
I came to be within the waters
of my mother's womb. So when I wash
I like to remember that I am in my element...
Your water...Your living water.
Help me scrub my face free of its masks
so I can return to the true self You gave me.

Let my hands not be afraid of dirt,
but let them come clean in obedience to You.

When I wash, let me recall the Well
where the water is.

Making the Bed

Plumping the pillow. Pulling on the sheets.
The bed reminds me that I am creating
my future every moment.

If I leave a mess, I will find what I left
sooner or later. I will not be exonerated
from any of my actions—
though knowing Your love, I will be forgiven much.

Here is a good place to pray.
I ask that You remind me in making the bed
to care for the future in the present,
being mindful also of my deathbed.

Help me to treasure this moment
which always returns me,
now and at the end, to You.

Choosing What to Wear

Is it a pink day, sky blue,
bottle green, or black?
I look in the closet. What kind of day is it?
I want to respond to this day,
to feel my "yes" to its color.

I stand by the closet door
barefooted before this choice.
When I pick now I want to remember
that You have picked me—
no self-made woman, but one brought forth
by the lives that have gone before me,
lives that have made mine possible...
from the first single-celled creatures,
those ancient ancestors,
to the dear ones I call parents.

Riches upon riches. Life shimmering forward.
Let me wear that ongoing color!
Let me wear the joy that matches this day.

Getting Dressed

You have made us so naked.
We have no plumage to speak of—no fur
or feathers against the cold. Does that mean
you want us to dress ourselves in nakedness?
To have only thin skins between us and You,
between us and Your world?

When I contemplate such nakedness
I know I cannot bear it.
I want immediately to cover myself.
Even so, You have placed Your life
within this exposed skin on purpose.
You have asked me to feel with You...
to be profoundly touched.

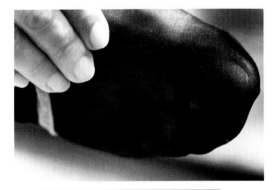

Let my need for safety not make
layers of insulation against the majesty
of Your trust in my vulnerability.
As I put on these clothes today let me remember
the intimate life You have called me to:
to touch and to be touched.
I don't want to shy away from knowing this
when I am with others. Let me wear
these outer garments lightly...for warmth
and for shelter...within them, let me remain
as you made me...utterly naked.

Looking in the Mirror

When I look in the mirror
let me try to see what You see—
the self You gave me to be.
Let me find the courage to carry
both the dark and the light of it.

In whatever small ways I can,
let me mirror Your will.

Crossing the Threshold

Many times today I will cross over a threshold.
I hope I will catch a few of those times.
I need to remember that my life is, in fact,
a continuous series of thresholds:
from one moment to the next,
from one thought to the next,
from one action to the next.

Help me appreciate how awesome this is.
How many are the chances to be really alive...
to be aware of the enormous dimension
we live within.

On the threshold the entire past
and the endless future
rush to meet one another.

They take hold of each other and laugh.
They are so happy to discover themselves
in the awareness of a human creature.
On the threshold the present breaks all boundaries.
It is a convergence,
a fellowship with all time and space.
We find You there.
And we are found by You there.

Help me cross into the present moment—
into wonder, into Your grace:
that "now-place," where we all are,
unfolding as Your life moment by moment.

Let me live on the threshold as threshold.

Climbing Stairs

I climb downstairs to the first floor
and I think of ladders...the one that Jacob saw
with the angels going up and down...the one
rising out of the kiva...the one against
the burning building on the evening news.

Help me to not be so afraid
of the heights and depths! Help me
to concentrate on the connection
between the two: those humble steps,
those one-after-the-other steps,
which are the only ones I can really take.
Help me to love a slow progression,
to have no prejudice
that up is better than down or vice versa.
Help me to enjoy the in-between.

Standing here on the first floor I remember
going down the stairs on my bottom
as a toddler. *Thud...thud...thud...*
It was energizing.
I want to reclaim bumping along again....
Please keep me from all spiritual ambition!

Breakfast

I gaze at this brown breakfast egg.
It is still warm from boiling.
Freckled, it is a presence here
on the counter...a *particular* egg.
And I will soon eat it.

My mind goes to nourishment—
of the body, yes—but also the other kind.
How often it seems I have to be in trouble
before I will let in the compassion I need
to live a human life.
When I discover in myself, finally,
a deep willingness to receive nourishment,
something has to change in me.
In some alchemical way, I know
I will have to become the nourishment
I sought in the first place.
And the shell will have to crack,
will have to be offered up.

A not-so-simple egg!
As I eat, let me digest this mystery.

Opening the Window

The window slides down on its track—
swings open on its hinge—
rises like the skylight. In comes the air,
rushing! Suddenly inside and outside are one.
This happens too fast for evaluation.

Already, before thought,
I am smelling winter...
cold wet earth and something
astringently joyous. I am feeling winter.
It is a blue cold, a happy crackling cold,
a shouting cold. I am struck by it
...wakened...gladdened.

Please open me like this window to the joy
that is always right here, beyond thought.
Help me feel that cruel-to-my-ego,
infallible love that fills me with fresh air.
Jolt me open to joy.

Planning the Day

The lists grow—
sometimes on lengthy strips of paper.
How easily my life becomes a list—
a long scroll of duties.

Sometimes the lists break down
into separate memos—
A batch of yellow memory scraps
each with an injunction.
Do this! Do that!

I can't get rid of my lists.

Perhaps there is some primitive magic here,
that if I name my duties I *must* perform them.
But then I almost always rebel.
These lists when they aren't burdening me,
give me an oppositional determination
to disobey and to do whatever I please.

Why do I put this "have-to-do-it" burden
on myself? It only makes me righteous,
artificially safe, and soul-tired.

Help me to sit here quietly.
Help me not so much to plan as to *listen*.
Help me to be informed, as in
"shaped from within," by Your will.
My burden is so heavy.
Yours is always light.

Sweeping

It's an old friend, this broom.
I like how it is made—
all these bits of brush sewn into one tool.
Together with the handle and my arms,
this becomes a unit
which can move sand and dirt.

I like joining this tool.
The arms move, the handle moves,
the broom head moves,
the dirt moves up and over the threshold.

We are sweeping—a kind of delicate dance
which results in this dirt being outside
now with the other dirt—moved on.
I want to be here with this moving on,
moment to moment, sweeping.

Let my concentration be the handle;
my body's effort, the will;
the broom head like my thoughts
coming together into one willingness—
moving on, moving on—
not clinging to anything.

The foyer is tidier and my inner mudroom
more at peace. I am returned to You.
A clean sweep.

Dusting

Time to dust again.
Time to caress my house,
to stroke all its surfaces.
I want to think of it as a kind of lovemaking
...the chance to appreciate by touch
what I live with and cherish.

The rags come out—old soft pajama legs,
torn undershirts, frayed towels.
They are still of use.
It is precisely because they have exhausted
their original use that they have come
to this honorable task.

Rag in hand, I feel along each piece
of furniture I live with, and luster returns
to the old sideboard, to the chair legs
and the lamp stands. It is as if by touch
they are revealed and restored to themselves.
Strange that in the dumbness of inanimate things
one can feel so much silent response.
What then of us animate creatures?

We are so many-surfaced: bumpy, smooth,
prickly, rough, silky, hairy, spiny, soft, scaly,
furry, feathery, sharp, and on and on.
And don't we all want to be stroked in some way
...to be restored to ourselves by touch
as much as by sight or smell or sound?

I want to be a lover of surfaces all day today.
Let this be the prayer:
that my hands not be ashamed
to give and to receive a passionate exchange
...to luster and to be lustered...
and so come to feel Your inward touch.

Taking Out the Trash

The trash bin is overflowing under the sink.
It's time to feed the big outdoor garbage can
again. How quickly it happens...how astonishing
that every week my bins are full to the brim
with the wastes of my daily existence.
Here I am dumping everything
from carrot peelings to junk mail.
What a mess I make!

I try to remember that You planned waste
as an essential part of life. It, too, is holy.
I want to keep in mind
the pine tree by the front door
and how it keeps dropping its numberless needles
—a tall and humble prayer.

I want to shed my waste with quiet reverence
like the pine. I want somehow to have a
conscience, a responsibility, for what it means
personally, socially, and ecologically to have
this much trash EVERY WEEK.
Help me to stop this hurry
to get my psychological and actual trash
out of sight and out of mind
and learn instead.

This task is a kind of surrender...
surrender to the knowledge that by being alive
and human I do make a human mess
as a pine tree makes its kind of mess.
Let me surrender any fake and pristine sense
of not affecting my fellow beings
and my environment with my waste.
Let me own my part of the landfill...
the one outside of town with the bulldozer
and the psychological one we all share.

Keep me mindful of what I take
into my home, the items bought to substitute
for real living—the food and drink I consume
instead of examining my feelings.
Help me slowly to surrender all excess.

Sorting Wash

Out of the hamper onto the floor,
the wash lies in a heap and I must sort
the dark clothes from the light, the delicate
from the ordinary before they are washed.

Categories—I think about how much
we use them. This is not that. This belongs.
That does not. We cannot do without sorting,
without categories, without definitions.
Even in this activity I know that without sorting
the colors could bleed in the wash.
They have to be separated according to kind.

In how many countless situations
have I named, separated, and judged
instead of celebrated.
In how many ways have I observed,
evaluated, sorted, and pulled away.
My preferences rule me.

Amidst this pile of wash I want to learn again
to participate and to be open to difference:
to celebrate the dark, to honor the light,
to bow to the delicate as well as the sturdy,
to appreciate texture and weight. To be
more equally with the various and the strange.

Soon the clothes will be drenched
in water and soap.
It will be a different time,
and sorting will no longer matter
in the midst of the wash cycle.
I need to learn this in life:
when to recognize, to name, and to sort—
and when to immerse, to soak, to tumble,
and be rinsed free of opinions.
Grant that I may as much as possible
honor You in all things.

Repotting

How hard it is to know
when the pot is too small for the plant.
Some plants need to be contained, held very close.
Others cannot be crowded.
I don't know when I myself am too pot-bound,
lacking courage to be replanted,
to take the shock of new soil,
to feel into the unknown and to take root in it.

This drying out, this self-crowding
sneaks up on me. It seems I must always feel
a little wilted or deadened before I know
I'm too pot-bound.

This african violet must first be cut
and divided. The knife goes through the root.
The white flesh exposed and moist
looks as if it is bleeding.
It must have soil immediately
so the plant won't die.
Then water. Water taken in from below.
This water must seep up into the plant
by infusion. Then comes the waiting
as the shock registers.
Days and weeks of waiting.

It will be months before a new leaf appears.
Perhaps the plant won't make it.
So it is when the time comes for me to be cut
and divided so as to grow again.

Help me to see this not as a problem
but as a process. Help me surrender
to the growth that only comes with pain,
with division, with helplessness, with waiting.
Especially the days and weeks of waiting.

Polishing the Silver

My fingers are full of dark smudges
polishing this silver. It looks good.
I can see my face in the soup ladle.
How I *do* like to look good to myself!
And the cost is always some kind of dirt
on my hands, some kind of slavery.

More polish on the rag. What kind of effort
is this really? I hold these old family objects
that so many hands have held. How strange
to know that this good silver
will outlast my life and my children's lives.

Here, around each of us
are the things we live with.
They are like tracks an animal leaves behind
that show where it has been.
How insignificant we let ourselves become
beside our things when we allow them
to stand for us, to be the sum of our existence.

As I polish let me remember
the fleeting time I am here. Let me let go of
all silver. Let me enter this moment
and polish it bright. Let me not lose my life
in any slavery—from looking good
to preserving the past, to whatever idolatry
that keeps me from just this—
the grateful receiving of the next thing at hand.

Paying Bills

Here are the bills again.
I always dread them a little.
They are familiar presences:
first in the mail box, then in the bill drawer,
now on the desk. Services Rendered.
My life is dependent on services rendered.

Somehow I am glad to pay Richard
for the plowing, Chic for the plumbing,
Walter for fixing the roof. I know them.
They make my life possible.
It is harder to pay the faceless ones
—the ones behind these white envelopes.
Here are the lives behind the heat,
the light, the telephone
—behind the counters and computers.
I want to learn to feel a friendliness toward them.
I want to acknowledge them.

When I write my checks I want to feel
that I am returning energy in the form of money
for energy given in the form of service.
It is all Your energy. We are only each other's way
to share in that great service which is Your life
poured out continually for us all without exception.

Guard me against the arrogance of privilege,
against the indulgence of feeling
that I don't have enough, and the poverty of spirit
that refuses to acknowledge what is
daily given me. Keep me truthful in knowing
where I spend, where my values actually are.

Let me not skip this monthly knowing.
Instruct me in judicious spending
and in gratitude with no holds barred.
I want always to give thanks and acknowledgment
to the ones I know who help my life
and to the faceless ones whom I will never know.

Hanging Out the Clothes

As I hang up these clothes let me think
about what it means to be "on the line."
It may not be about courage or bravery
or intention. It may not be about social action,
good works, or justice. It may be
something before that, something much earlier,
more simple and humbling.

It may just be about clinging for dear life.

I pin these wet clothes to the line...
an image of joining, of clinging *to* something.
If I really know that You are my lifeline
then to cling to You is my primary business.

There are so many spiritual traps
if I am the one who puts me on the line.
Instead, let me be simpler, let me just cling to You.

Then all the other lines in my life fall in place:
the line of duty, the line of business,
the line of poetry, the firing line.
Please help me to cling so tenaciously
that I find myself in line with You—
aired out and shaken.

Reading the Paper

The terrible fascinates.
This reading of the paper trains my fear.
I can feel it.
I want to know the disaster even as I recoil.
I am not separate from the deaths, the demands,
and the dealings, the disasters, the deceits,
the demagogues, and the diplomats.

This is *our* incompleteness, our separation,
our greed at work. Let me own my part.
The world's hunger is mine.
The world's helplessness is mine.
The world's failure to love is mine.
Sober me to this connection in my life.
Let the news be printed on my conscience.
Help me bear it.

Listening

Somehow, I must sit to listen.
Standing implies the readiness for action,
for the executing of the will.
To hear You I must sit down and calm down.

The magpie mind chatters.
It doesn't know about stopping.
How helpless I feel in its automatic firing,
its busy babbling. It is impossible to hear You
as long as I am full of sound.
I turn this helpless prayer toward You.
Help me to be quiet, to sit here
...slowly unknowing everything,
becoming dark, becoming yielding...
just sitting.

Here, without will, let me become willing.
Here, without concepts, help me to know.
Here, without doing, turn me toward usefulness.
Let my heart find its ears in You.
Let the countless cells of my body
open in order to listen,
Let my being come into Your presence
and experience the sound of Your light.

Shoveling

The snow comes down in heaps.
All that white mess. It's beautiful.
But when I look at it now, I see
only INCONVENIENCE. How much
of Your world do I regard in this way?
Why is it so hard to live with
the beauty of "the way things are"?

I'm always wanting my own weather.
Instead, here are six inches of white stuff
to glower at. I bundle up and begin the task
of making navigable trails.
The shovel rises and falls.
I am getting heated.

How many things do I shovel aside?
How many ways do I have to pile things up
out of my way? I am always arranging
instead of appreciating.

I want to feel a proper shame.
You've made every snowflake
in its own pattern. Not one is the same.
Here they are six inches deep!
Each an individual.
How precise and abundant are the forms
You have given Your creatures.
How staggering is Your care.

The snow is shimmering from within itself.
It has a pale blue light...
the confidence of its own nature.
And now despite myself, I feel
You turning my complaint into begrudging praise.

I am grateful that You give me
these new eyes to see Your joy,
even as it sky-rides into my backyard
and forces me to come to grips with it.

Laying a Fire

Old newspapers rolled into butterflies—
a black-and-white nest of them.
Then comes the kindling—bits of this and that
gathered and placed on the paper. Last, the logs.
The fire is laid and is without flame.

So often I am waiting like this, unlit,
longing for Your presence.
I can find the discipline, by habit mostly,
to lay a readiness inside myself.
But until You strike the match
there is no passion, no heat.
Without You I am a dark thing, unkindled.

Let me be content to watch
for the stirring of Your flame.
Let me learn to be ready, to wait,
to have no light.
Help me trust that this, too, is obedience
...that flamelessness can also be
a kind of burning.

Paperwork

The papers make a loose and messy nest
on my desk. I know there is an order here
but it will not show itself.
I must allow myself to be impressed
by what exists on the surface,
to let the work introduce itself.

It is as if I were talking to a stranger
who is slowly becoming known to me.
What is first shared does not always
reveal the truth. Under the obvious,
the real task can be hiding
its radiance, its meaning and pain.

If I don't continually meet my work like this
I will assume things. I will be automatic,
a robot, just doing, forgetting also to be.
The work asks me to be in relationship with it.
It wants me to be equal to it and with it.
When I find that mutuality, the doing can start.
Then the order which has been waiting to emerge,
which wanted me to find it,
begins to show itself.

The real work is revealed
and I am discovered by the work.
We are found in each other and released beyond ourselves.
This is grace.
I thank You for the potential of this each day.
How marvelous that a nest of papers can be
a place where new things come to be.

Taking a Breather

Exhaling, I feel the breath leave me.
When it is cold
I can see this bit of personal steam
escaping into the air.

Now...if I wait patiently...
the breath will remember to come back.
It will return with my life. Over and over
my life is returned like this
because You are breathing me.

This gift is given to me countless times a day.
All I have to do is remember!

Arranging Flowers

I put these tulips in a simple vase.
They are white, virginal, so themselves
that they remind me of nakedness, of truth.
The petals are opening—creamy and heavy.
These tulips are in full bloom
and they will wither.

Their life is no different from mine,
but to bear that life with consciousness
is so difficult.

When I allow myself to commune
with these flowers, I know
I am asked to come into fragrance and fruition
...to blossom fully and then to let go.
Like these flowers I am blooming and dying.
How mysterious this is.
I bow to you, tulips.

Folding Clothes

Out of the dryer the clothes come
smelling of soap and fabric softener.
The underpants cling to the nightshirt.
The towels crackle.
Everything is mixed up with everything else.

I want to turn this heap
of electrical excitement
into some kind of order.
I want it to become
a means of prayer, a litany.

The hand towels come first.
Each day a new one goes on the hook.
Let the folding of these towels
be an invocation. I think of the hands
that have been dried on them.
Tentative, strong, confused, determined hands.
Grant that our hands will find ways
to do Your will. Keep us in Your love.

Now the sheets.
My friends slept in them last night.
Let the folding of these sheets
be an intercession. Fold my friends
into Your tenderness. Keep us in Your love.

Then the personal clothes.
One sock is rolled together with its mate.
One sweater sleeve goes over the other,
an image of repose.
Let the folding of these garments
be a confession. Help me to surrender,
to give up all those false excitements,
clinging attachments, static insistencies.
Help me instead to be folded into You.
Help me to be clothed by You, to dwell in You,
to make my life an obedience.
Keep us in Your love.

Let the completed task be offered...
such a small thing...yet let it be offered
as thanksgiving. Your amazing mystery is here
even now receiving this smallness.
Keep us in Your love.

Ironing

The iron heats up. The board unfolds and
stands like a free-form sculpture on the floor.
In the basket lies the wash,
rolled and sprinkled.
Moisture hangs in the air,
a clean and steamy fragrance.

Soon the iron will hiss and glide,
will flatten these shirts and give them a shape,
sharp creases, crisp collars, smooth cuffs.

My hand glides with the iron.
Under this heat the cloth begins to lie flat,
pressed. To iron things out...
I think of how easily acts of management
can slide into power. In one instant
of believing that I know best,
I can place myself outside of Your mercy.
The crease will be in the wrong place.

Help me to remember how You love
the crumpled as much as the smooth.
In You they are one.
These clothes will all be wrinkled again,
like my life—crumpled and ordered
and crumpled again.

Make my hand light. Help me remember
You are the giver of shapes
whose mercy orders all things.

Turning on the Light

Without this darkness—no awareness of light.
Without this light—no awareness of darkness.
In the flickering of the flame,
in the delicate filament of the bulb
is the light that is also the dark,
the dark that is also the light.

I shall never understand this mystery.
Light and dark are somehow the same.
I want not to prefer one over the other
but to appreciate their unique
and simultaneous truth.

Now light. Now dark. The switch turns,
the wick catches fire. In that split second
dark and light are one
as is everything in the universe.
Every moment we live in split-second reality
as unique and simultaneous truths. We are one
and together because of each other,
with each other,
for each other.
We are Your glory leaping into itself.
And we don't even know it!

When the light switch turns let me feel
how my small life leaps into being in the One Life,
the way a flame becomes itself in the fire.
My life has known how to do this
from the start. It wants to do it.
Help me live what is already true.
Help me to know it.

Straightening the Cupboard

Cans of soup, packages of pasta, tins of tea,
flour, salt, and sugar.
I wipe down the shelf and line up the staples again.
There is comfort here and danger.
When I look into this well-stocked cupboard
I can sense the temptation to think I am secure...
a secret pride in "what I am able to provide."
Some of these cans have been here a long time.
Am I secretly hoarding?

I can reach for any of this at will.
Before I even open the cupboard,
before anything, help me to reach for You.
My pride is silly.
The hoarding, a lack of trust.
There is no supply outside of You.

You are the daily abundance, poured out.
Empty me to receive You each day.

Setting the Table

As I lay the fork near the plate,
let me remember this is Your table, not mine.
As I set the water glasses down
and fold the napkins, let me be reminded
that every setting at this table
is Yours, not mine.

Each one who will partake of this meal
is a particular someone You love, a someone
You have made and whom You sustain.
In You nothing and no one is forgotten.
How vast and providential is the memory
with which You keep us all.

It is only we who forget You
and then one another.
It is we who starve each other
and exclude each other.
Give me new eyes.
When the glass is raised by my friend
let me see You drinking.
When the fork is lifted by my child,
let me recognize You eating.
You are the hidden joy which feeds
and keeps everything. You are the table,
the guest, the meal, and the commemoration.

Make in my person a place setting for You.
Remind me of my true nature
which is recalled only in You.

Cooking

Peeling, chopping, cutting, mincing, slicing,
measuring, pouring, stirring, poaching,
bubbling, frying, turning, simmering, serving.
These are words I cook with.
They are all motion, all process.

I know as I create this meal
there is another cooking going on.
It, too, is all motion, all process—
an inner transformation.
Help me to give myself away
as easily as this carrot, this new potato.
I want my layers to peel away like the onion's.
I want to be as empty and clean
as the universe in a sweet green pepper
with its white star seeds.

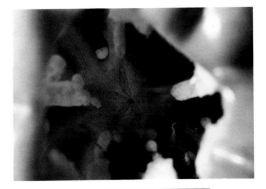

I want. I want. In the heat of Your will
help me to give up wanting!
I am so full of urgency, expectation, image,
I make myself spiritually hungry. You are here,
therefore, there is everything to receive.

Saying Grace

Here is supper. It smells good.
It looks good. It tastes good.
It is good.
All good things come from You.

Let the sweet taste of You
become the constant blessing on my tongue.

Doing the Dishes

My life will always have dirty dishes.
If this sink can become
a place of contemplation,
let me learn constancy here.

I gaze through the window above the sink.
There I see the constancy of dawn,
the constancy of dusk,
the constancy of the seasons,
of the sun and moon,
and the rotation of the planets.

Your love is discerned by repetition.
Turn and return me to Your love.
Let my fitful human constancy
be strengthened in the willing,
wheeling wonder of Your stars.

Mending

Holes in the fabric…tears
and unravelings. What can be mended?
What is rent for good?

I try to make decisions about this —
One garment cannot be fixed —
into the rag bag it goes!
But another can be stitched together again.

As I sort and mend I think of the larger fabric,
the fabric of life. I think about relationships
that tear apart. No amount of stitching will help.
No button can hold them together.
Sometimes what is torn needs to lie there —
frayed edges exposed, the gaping hole honored.

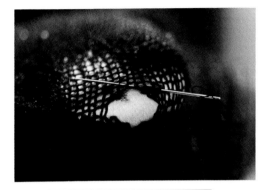

Teach me to be humble
when the patching goes wrong,
when I join parts that don't belong,
when the button still does not meet the hole.
Help me to realize when my busy needle
will do no good.

Not knowing what to do or what is right...
feeling this helplessness returns me to You.
Invisible, the thread is in Your hand.
Beyond knowing
what is torn apart breathes
in its own way with You,
mends if it can, when it can.
Let me accept the frayed.

Locking the Door

Nightfall...morning.
I lock the door. I unlock it.
My days are punctuated with this act.
It is a rhythm, a kind of pulse.

Just now the door is locked.
I want to think of this not as
shutting the world out or shutting me in.
I want to think of this more
like dwelling in a rhythm...
a sweet measure. Soon it will be morning
and the door will be unlocked again.

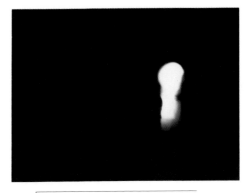

I can dwell in this home
as if it were a heart. When I feel that pulse
I know that all that comes to me will also go.
Living in this stream I understand
You are my life blood. Let me feel
You course through me, through this door,
throughout my life.

Setting the Alarm

The alarm is set. Good!

I know I am asleep—even now
while I walk around.
I am a somnambulist in the midst of life,
which is so terrible and sweet
that if I don't wake up I will miss it.

Whisper in my inner ear! Alert my eyes
to this night, these stars that shine
even in the day when I cannot see them.
Wake me to the real and radiant world.
My whole life depends on being awake!

Entering Rest

Dear Companion of my day,
You are the Holy Mystery I surrender to
when I close my eyes. I give You myself:
the flaws, the mistakes, the petty
self-congratulations. I give You my dear ones:
my fondest hopes for them, my worries,
and my dark thoughts regarding them.
Take my well-constructed separation from me.
Hold me in Your truth.

This day is already past. I surrender it.
When I think about tomorrow, I surrender it too.
Keep me this night. With You
and in You I can trust not knowing anything.
I can trust incompleteness as a way.
Dark with the darkness, silent with the silence,
help me dare to be that empty one—futureless,
desireless—who breathes Your name even in sleep.

Conclusion

One day...one whole day with its night passes. It is a whole lifetime, a wide and radiant gate into Mystery. It is staggering. An unbelievable gift. I am still too unconscious to receive it.

How do we receive this wonder? The only answer I can come up with for myself is to receive it in measured doses. My little consciousness cannot bear how vast the love is that holds my life. I must receive this love by quarter-teaspoons, by drops, by thimblefuls.

I am reminded of a woman I once worked with in therapy. She was a gardener yet could never quite become a gardener. Her life was one of pleasing others, revving through tasks to mask a deep self-doubt and anxiety. One day she came to the office with eyes like blue sapphires, like blue stars. She was on fire.

"Gunilla," she said, "today I can die. For one half hour I have lived. I gardened! The dirt, the trowel, the plants, the sky, the sun, the water—it was all inside me. I really gardened. I can die. Now I can die."

Her face and her truth are precious to me. To garden, to do the dishes, to make the bed, to sweep. To be here, to do what must be done. To really be with the Great Love whose life we are, we can die then; any moment, we can die, and we can live the wonder of a new day.

About the Author & the Photographer

Gretchen Tatge

Norman Sibley

Gunilla Norris lives in Newtown, Connecticut, where she works as a writer and psychotherapist in private practice. She is the author of eleven children's books and one book of poems, *Learning from the Angel*. Her special love is giving workshops on mindfulness and self-care for corporations and groups of all kinds.

Greta D. Sibley began her career twelve years ago in Seoul, Korea, where she and a handful of friends founded a magazine, published books, and ran a design agency. Her photographs have been exhibited at the National Museum of Modern Art in Seoul and at the Korean Cultural Center in Los Angeles. She returned to the United States in 1983 and has been working as a free-lance book designer ever since.

In 1986 Gunilla Norris and Greta Sibley began collaborating as editor and art director of Small Offerings, a press dedicated to the artistic expression of the spiritual impulse.

Being Home exists as an exhibit as well as in book form.